Giggle Fit™

Hilarious Halloween Jokes

Alison Grambs

Illustrated by Steve Harpster

Sterling Publishing Co., Inc. New York

Library of Congress Cataloging-in-Publication Data Available

10 9 8 7 6 5 4 3 2 1

Published by Sterling Publishing Co., Inc.
387 Park Avenue South, New York, NY 10016
© 2004 by Alison Grambs
Distributed in Canada by Sterling Publishing
%o Canadian Manda Group, One Atlantic Avenue, Suite 105
Toronto, Ontario, Canada M6K 3E7
Distributed in Great Britain and Europe by Chris Lloyd at Orca Book
Services, Stanley House, Fleets Lane, Poole BH15 3AJ, England
Distributed in Australia by Capricorn Link (Australia) Pty. Ltd.
P.O. Box 704, Windsor, NSW 2756, Australia

Manufactured in China
All rights reserved

Sterling ISBN 1-4027-1243-X

Knock-Knock.
Who's there?
Wart.
Wart who?
**Wart you like to come
trick-or-treating with me?**

When do cows go
trick-or-treating?
**During the full
mooooooooon.**

Knock-Knock.
Who's there?
Orange.
Orange who?
**Orange you glad I gave you
a treat and not a trick?**

What's Dracula's favorite holiday?
Fangsgiving.

What did Dracula and Jill carry to the top of the hill?
A pale and bucket.

Why did Dracula return his new computer to the store?
It didn't have enough bytes.

Did Dracula compete in the Olympics?
Yes, he even won the bite-athlon.

Why did Dracula become
a vegetarian?
**Because stake doesn't
agree with him.**

Do you think Dracula can get the job done?
Sure, he's very cape-able.

Why doesn't Dracula do well on blind dates?
Because all the girls think he's a little batty.

How do baby bears catch spiders?
In their cub-webs.

What do dogs dress up as
on Halloween?
Were-woofs.

How do bats fly at night
without directions?
**Oh, they usually just
wing it.**

What kind of snakes do ghosts fear most?
Boo-a constrictors.

What do spiders eat at barbecues?
Corn on the cobweb.

Why do chickens dread Halloween?
It's a night of bad pluck.

Why did the witch's broom have such a
bad first day at work?
It couldn't get a handle on things.

Why was the witch's broom tossing
and turning?
It was having trouble sweeping.

How can witches get
rid of brooms they
don't need anymore?
Sale-m.

Why did the witch crash her broom?
Because she fell a-sweep while flying.

Why did the witch buy a new broom?
The one she had didn't handle well in the winter.

Why did the witch sell her broom for so little money?
Because it wasn't wart that much in the first place.

Why was the ghost wearing a Band-Aid?
Because he had a boo-boo.

Knock-Knock.
Who's there?
Goblin.
Goblin who?
Goblin all your food up at once will only give you a tummy ache.

How does a monster treat a sore throat?
It gargoyles with mouthwash.

Knock-Knock.
  Who's there?
Irvin.
  Irvin who?
Irvin if it's bad for your teeth, candy tastes yummy!

Why is it easy to catch
a cold in a cemetery?
  **Because there's a lot
  of coffin.**

Knock-Knock.
  Who's there?
Owl.
  Owl who?
Owl, that werewolf bit me!

Why was the boy witch unable to go out?
His parents kept him under warlock and key.

Why did the little witch get
in trouble with the big witch?
**Because she got caught
cursing.**

Why did the zombie get
detention?
**Because he was late
for ghoul.**

Why was the werewolf upset?
A cop gave him a barking ticket.

How do vampire police find the bad guys?
They go on stake-outs.

Why were the mashed potatoes tossed in jail?
For grave-y robbing.

Why was the spirit pulled over on the highway?
The cop said he was ghosting too slowly.

How do goblins get around?

They take the troll-ey.

What were the trick-or-treaters doing at the gas station?

Pumpkin gas.

Why did the ghost stop his car before the bridge?

Because there was a toll boooooooth.

Was the movie about the possessed car good?

Yes, it was wheely, wheely scary!

What event can
Frankenstein simply not
miss each year?
**The Monster Truck
Show.**

What sound does a
witch's car make?
**Brooooom!
Broooooooom!**

Why was the werewolf
having trouble driving
on the road?
**Because the corners got
a bit hairy sometimes.**

Why did the warlock get lost
in the woods?
**Because he didn't know
witch way to go.**

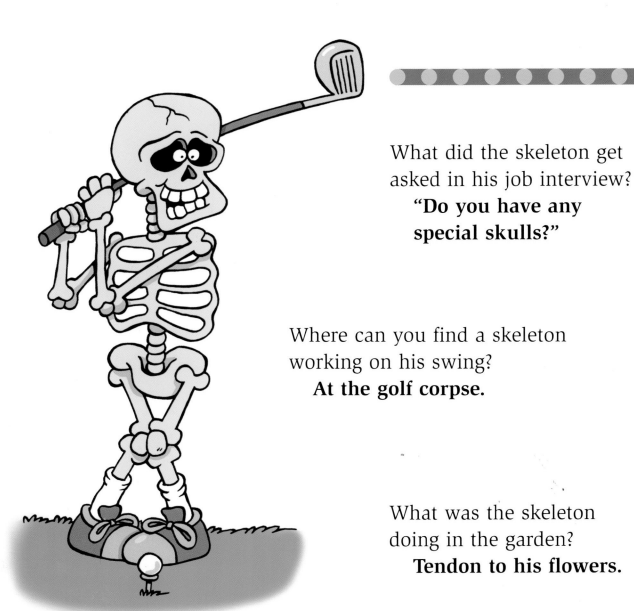

What did the skeleton get asked in his job interview?
"Do you have any special skulls?"

Where can you find a skeleton working on his swing?
At the golf corpse.

What was the skeleton doing in the garden?
Tendon to his flowers.

Why did the skeleton get sent to the principal's office?
Because it was late for skull.

Why was the skeleton studying so hard?
It wanted to get a-head in its studies.

Why do skeletons make great stand-up comedians?
Because they've got real funny bones.

What do skeletons wrap Christmas gifts with?
Pretty paper and rib-bons.

What holiday do zombies love most?
Mummy's Day.

What do mummies eat for
dinner every night?
Ghoul-lash.

Knock-Knock.
  Who's there?
Mummy.
  Mummy who?
**Mummy makes the
world go around!**

Why can't mummies cook?
Because tomb many cooks spoil the broth!

When is the mummy going
to the dentist?
Tomb-orrow.

What's a mummy's
favorite dinner?
**Spaghetti in
tomb-ato sauce.**

Why couldn't the werewolf go on vacation?
Because he didn't have any moon-ey.

Why doesn't anyone like the werewolf cheerleader?
Because she's sort of snouty.

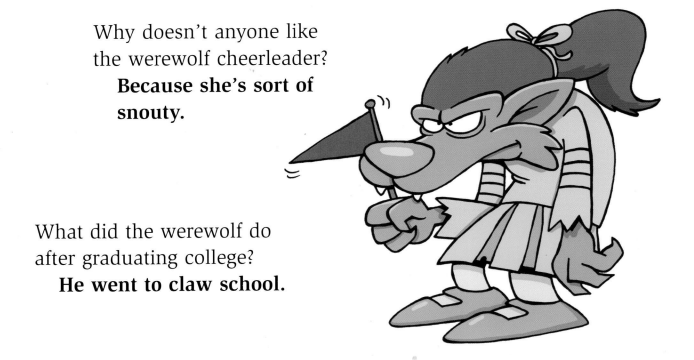

What did the werewolf do after graduating college?
He went to claw school.

What's the best way to greet a werewolf?
Say, "Hey! Howl you doin'?"

What kind of wolf is hard to locate?
A where wolf.

Why was the little werewolf failing English class?
Because he didn't know howl to spell very well.

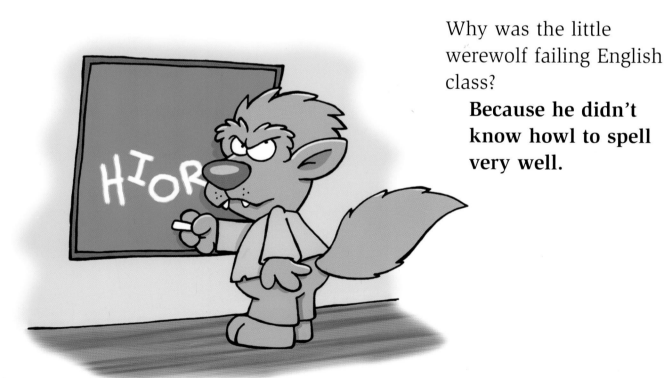

How do monsters keep the bugs out of their houses?
They put screams on the front door.

Were the neighbors finally able to sell their haunted house?
Nope, they didn't stand a ghost of a chance.

Knock-Knock.
Who's there?
Witch.
Witch who?
Witch way to the haunted house?

What's scarier than an uncle's house?
An aunt-ed house.

How does a ghost get into a house?
It uses a spook-key.

What do horse racers decorate their homes with on Halloween?
Jockey-lanterns.

What do you do when a pumpkin arrives at your house for dinner?
Offer him a seed in the living room.

Knock-Knock.
Who's there?
Ghost.
Ghost who?
Ghost slowly when you walk through a haunted house.

What do vampires carry their books in at school?
Knap-sucks.

Are witches good in math?
Of curse they are!

How do spiders do computer research?
On the Web.

What does Dracula look for
at the library?
**Books he can really
sink his teeth into.**

Is the little witch good
in school?
**Yes, her favorite
subject is spelling.**

How did the jack-o-lantern get into the best school?
**His teacher gave him a glowing
recommendation.**

What does a ghost do when he runs out of milk?
Ghost to the supermarket just like everyone else!

What do Australian ghosts hunt with?
Boo-merangs.

Why do ghosts make good cheerleaders?
Because they have a lot of spirit.

What do you call it when
Halloween spirits rob a bank?
A polter-heist.

What do you call ghosts born
during World War II?
Baby Booooomers.

What do old spirits do
when they retire?
**They move to a ghost
town.**

GHOUL # 1: Okay, I did that favor for you.
GHOUL # 2: Wow, I'm forever in-deaded to
you!

Why did Dracula win the beauty pageant?
Because the other contestants paled in comparison to him.

Why are mummies so self-centered?
Because they tend to get wrapped up in themselves.

Are female ghosts attractive?
Yes, they're quite boo-tiful.

Why do mummies go to the beauty salon?
To have their hair died.

Where do vampires fly to for a vacation by the sea?
Cape Cod.

Where do ghosts go for baked beans?
Boo-ston, Massachusetts.

Why couldn't the witch stay on vacation?
There wasn't any broom at the hotel.

What kind of whale haunts France?
The Humpback of Notre Dame.

What do skeletons fry their eggs in?
A skull-et.

What does an apple pie's headstone say?
Rest in piece.

What are they serving for dessert on Halloween this year?
I scream and cake.

What does a skeleton eat at a picnic?
Barbecued ribs.

What's a tasty treat at cemeteries?
Straw-burries and cream.

What's another tasty treat at cemeteries?
Mashed potatoes and grave-y.

Why do monsters like
to eat bananas?
**Because they find
them very
a-peeling.**

How do you know a piece of Halloween candy has a crush on you?

It acts all sweet.

Knock-Knock.
Who's there?
Mustache.
Mustache who?
Mustache your candy away so no one else eats it.

Knock-Knock.
Who's there.
Bats.
Bats who?
Bats my candy, not yours!

Why don't kids like chocolate
cookies on Halloween?
**Because they have a real
chip on their shoulders.**

What Halloween treat is never on time?
Choco-late.

Where do candied apples volunteer?
In the peace core.

Why was the little witch crying at the dinner table?
Because she spelled the milk.

Do witches eat a lot?
No, actually, they eat pretty small potions.

What do witches eat at barbecues?
Halloweenies and fries.

What do witches order at hotels
when they get hungry?
Broom service.

What contests do witches
always win?
Spell-ing bees.

Where do witches play golf?
On a golf curse.

What baseball position
does Dracula play?
Batter.

What other baseball position
does Dracula play?
Vumpire.

What football position does Dracula play?
Quarterbat.

Which ghoul won the race?
Actually, it was a dead tie.

Why was Dracula told to stop playing tennis?
Because he was making too much of a racket.

Where do zombies swim?
In a swimming ghoul.

Knock-Knock.
Who's there?
Troll.
Troll who?
Troll me the ball and I'll catch it.

What musical instrument do skeletons enjoy playing?
The trom-bone.

What chorus do goblins sing on
Christmas Eve?
Troll-lalalalalalalalala.

What brand of piano do
monsters play?
The Frankensteinway.

What do skeletons sing into at a karaoke party?
A micro-bone.

Why did the witch stop singing along with the CD?
She forgot the warts to the song.

What classical composer do witches listen to on their broom radios?
Handel.

Why was the goblin annoyed on his road trip?
Because he had to pay a troll at the bridge.

Why were the ghosts upset?
Because their party guests were goblin up all the potato chips.

How do you know a skeleton is depressed?
It's seen skull-king around a lot.

Are homemade Halloween costumes difficult to make?
Yes, they're the harvest ones of all.

What do ghosts wear with their jeans?
Boo-ts.

What T-shirts do zombies absolutely love?
Tie-died ones.

What kind of sweater does Dracula wear?
Afraid one.

What do mummies wear to school when it's raining?
Their ghoul-ashes.

41

Knock-Knock.
  Who's there?
Ivana.
  Ivana who?
Ivana get back to my coffin before day-break.

How do vampires get around?
  They ride bite-cycles.

Where do vampires go to wash?
  The bat-tub.

How does a vampiress flirt with a vampire?
  She bats her eyelashes at him.

How do vampires like their candy?
  In bite-size pieces.

Knock-Knock.
Who's there?
Bobby.
Bobby who?
Bobby for apples is my favorite Halloween game.

Knock-Knock.
Who's there?
Fall.
Fall who?
Fall me, I know a shortcut to the Halloween party.

Was Frankenstein in a rush to leave the party?
Yes, he bolted out of there.

What do vampires celebrate every two hundred years?
The bite-centennial.

Why are mummies so boring at parties?
Because they're very stiff.

Why was the grave digger running through the cemetery?

He was in a real bury.

Why did the sandwich end up in a cemetery?

He was bread and buried.

How do you split a tombstone in half?

You RIP it.

Why are books about cemeteries so boring?

They have weak plots.

Did the ghoul give you good directions to the cemetery?

Yes, they were dead on.

What should you do when a ghost can't understand what you say?

Spook a little more slowly.

Knock-Knock.
　Who's there?
Mask.
　Mask who?
Mask me a question, I'll tell you no lies.

Where do ghosts make calls?
In a phone boooooo-th.

How do you greet a pumpkin?
You say, "Hollow."

Knock-Knock.
Who's there?
Fangs.
Fangs who?
Fangs for the memories.

Knock-Knock.
Who's there?
Leaf.
Leaf who?
Leaf now, before the ghost gets you!

Knock-Knock.
Who's there?
Witch.
Witch who?
Witch on a star and your dreams might come true.

Knock-Knock.
Who's there?
Bats.
Bats who?
Bats all, folks!

INDEX

Apple pie, 30
Apples, 33, 43

Baked beans, 29
Bananas, 31
Band-Aid, 10
Banks, 27
Barbecues, 7, 34
Baseball, 36
Bats, 6, 32, 47
Bears, baby, 6
Beauty pageant, 28
Beauty salons, 28
Blind dates, 5
Bobby, 43
Books, 24, 25, 44
Brooms, 8–9, 39
Bugs, 22

Candy, 11, 32, 33, 42
Cars, 14, 15
Cemeteries, 11, 31, 44
Cheerleaders, 20, 26
Chickens, 7
Christmas gifts, 17
College, 20
Comedians, 17
Computers, 4, 24
Contests, 35
Cookies, 33
Costumes, 41
Cows, 3

Dentist, 19
Dessert, 30
Detention, 12
Dinner, 23

Dogs, 6
Dracula, 4–5, 25, 28, 36, 37, 41

Eggs, 30
English class, 21

Fall, 43
Fangs, 46
Food, 19, 29, 30–35
Football, 36
France, 29
Frankenstein, 15, 38, 43

Garden, 16
Gas stations, 14
Ghosts, 7, 10, 14, 23, 26, 27, 28, 29, 40, 41, 45
Ghouls, 27, 36, 44
Goblins, 10, 14, 38, 40
Golf, 16, 35
Grave digger, 44

Haunted houses, 22–23
Headstone, 30
Holidays, 4, 18
Horse racers, 23
Hotels, 35

Irvin, 11
Ivana, 42

Jack-o-lanterns, 25
Jeans, 41
Job interview, 16

Leaf, 46
Library, 25

Mashed potatoes, 13
Mask, 45
Math, 24
Milk, 26, 34
Monsters, 10, 15, 22, 31, 38
Movies, 14
Mummies, 18–19, 28, 41, 43
Music, 38–39
Mustache, 32

Olympics, 4
Orange, 3
Owl, 11

Parties, 40, 43
Pianos, 38
Picnics, 30
Police, 13
Principal's office, 17
Pumpkins, 23, 45

Road trip, 40

Sandwich, 44
School, 12, 17, 21, 24–25, 41
Singing, 38, 39
Skeletons, 16–17, 30, 38, 39, 40
Snakes, 7
Spells, 34
Spiders, 6, 7

Spirits, 13, 24, 27
Sports, 16, 35, 36–37
Sweater, 41
Swimming, 37

Tee-shirts, 41
Tennis, 37
Tombstone, 44
Trick-or-treaters, 3, 14
Trolls, 37, 40
Trucks, 15

Uncles, 23

Vacations, 20, 29
Vampire police, 13
Vampires, 24, 29, 42, 43
Vegetarian, 5

Warlocks, 12, 15
Wart(s), 3, 39
Werewolves, 13, 15, 20–21
Whales, 29
Witches, 8–9, 12, 15, 22, 24, 29, 34–35, 39, 47
Woods, 15
World War II, 27

Zombies, 12, 18, 37, 41